United States Government Accountability Office

GAO

Testimony
Before the Committee on Homeland
Security and Governmental Affairs,
U.S. Senate

For Release on Delivery
Expected at 10 a.m. EDT
Thursday, March 21, 2013

HIGH-RISK SERIES

I0448879

Government-wide 2013 Update and Progress Made by the Department of Homeland Security

Statement of Gene L. Dodaro
Comptroller General of the United States

GAO
Accountability * Integrity * Reliability

GAO-13-444T

Highlights of GAO-13-444T, a testimony
before the Committee on Homeland Security
and Governmental Affairs, U.S. Senate

HIGH-RISK SERIES

Government-wide 2013 Update and Progress Made by the Department of Homeland Security

Why GAO Did This Study

The federal government is a large and complex entity, with about $3.5 trillion in outlays in fiscal year 2012 funding a broad array of programs and operations. GAO maintains a program to focus attention on government operations that it identifies as high risk due to their greater vulnerabilities to fraud, waste, abuse, and mismanagement or the need for transformation to address economy, efficiency, or effectiveness challenges. Since 1990, more than one-third of the areas previously designated as high risk have been removed from the list because sufficient progress was made to address the problems identified.

The biennial high risk update describes the status of high-risk areas listed in 2011 and identifies any new high-risk area needing attention by Congress and the executive branch. Solutions to high-risk problems offer the potential to save billions of dollars, improve service to the public, and strengthen the performance and accountability of the U.S. government.

What GAO Recommends

The high risk report contains GAO's views on progress made and what remains to be done to bring about lasting solutions for each high-risk area. Perseverance by the executive branch in implementing GAO's recommended solutions and continued oversight and action by Congress are essential to achieving progress. GAO is dedicated to continue working with Congress and the executive branch to help ensure additional progress is made.

View GAO-13-444T. For more information, contact J. Christopher Mihm at (202) 512-6806 or mihmj@gao.gov, and Cathleen A. Berrick, (202) 512-3404 or berrickc@gao.gov.

What GAO Found

In the past 2 years, notable progress has been made in the vast majority of areas that were on GAO's 2011 High Risk List. Congress passed several laws and took oversight actions to help address high-risk areas. Top administration officials at the Office of Management and Budget and the individual agencies have continued to show their commitment to ensuring that high-risk areas receive attention and action. Additional progress is both possible and needed in all the high-risk areas on GAO's 2013 list.

Sufficient progress has been made to remove the high-risk designation from two high-risk areas on the 2011 list, *Management of Interagency Contracting* and *Internal Revenue Service Business Systems Modernization*. While these two areas have been removed from the list, GAO will continue to monitor them.

This year, GAO also has added two areas, *Limiting the Federal Government's Fiscal Exposure by Better Managing Climate Change Risks*, and *Mitigating Gaps in Weather Satellite Data*.

In 2003, GAO designated implementing and transforming the Department of Homeland Security (DHS) as high risk because DHS had to transform 22 agencies—several with major management challenges—into one department, and failure to address associated risks could have serious consequences. While challenges remain across its missions, DHS has made considerable progress in transforming its original component agencies into a single department. As a result, GAO narrowed the scope of the high-risk area and changed the name from *Implementing and Transforming the Department of Homeland Security* to *Strengthening the Department of Homeland Security Management Functions*.

To more fully address this high-risk area, DHS needs to further strengthen its acquisition, information technology, and financial and human capital management functions. Of the 31 actions and outcomes GAO identified as important to addressing this area, DHS has fully or mostly addressed 8, partially addressed 16, and initiated 7. Moving forward, DHS needs to, for example, do the following:

- *Acquisition management.* Validate required acquisition documents in a timely manner, and demonstrate measurable progress in meeting cost, schedule, and performance metrics for its major programs. GAO reported in September 2012, for example, that 42 major programs experienced cost growth, schedule slips, or both, and most programs lacked foundational documents needed to manage risk and measure performance.

- *Information technology management.* Demonstrate for at least two consecutive investment increments that actual cost and schedule performance is within established baselines, and that associated mission benefits have been achieved. DHS has begun to implement a governance structure to improve program management consistent with best practices, but the structure covers less than 20 percent of DHS's major information technology investments.

- *Financial management.* Achieve clean opinions for at least two consecutive years on departmentwide financial statements, and implement new or upgrade existing components' financial systems. DHS received a qualified opinion on its fiscal year 2012 financial statements, and is in the early planning stages of its financial systems modernization efforts.

GAO's 2013 High Risk List

Strengthening the Foundation for Efficiency and Effectiveness
- Limiting the Federal Government's Fiscal Exposure by Better Managing Climate Change Risks (new)
- Management of Federal Oil and Gas Resources
- Modernizing the U.S. Financial Regulatory System and Federal Role in Housing Finance
- Restructuring the U.S. Postal Service to Achieve Sustainable Financial Viability
- Funding the Nation's Surface Transportation System
- Strategic Human Capital Management
- Managing Federal Real Property

Transforming DOD Program Management
- DOD Approach to Business Transformation
- DOD Business Systems Modernization
- DOD Support Infrastructure Management
- DOD Financial Management
- DOD Supply Chain Management
- DOD Weapon Systems Acquisition

Ensuring Public Safety and Security
- Mitigating Gaps in Weather Satellite Data (new)
- Strengthening Department of Homeland Security Management Functions
- Establishing Effective Mechanisms for Sharing and Managing Terrorism-Related Information to Protect the Homeland
- Protecting the Federal Government's Information Systems and the Nation's Cyber Critical Infrastructures
- Ensuring the Effective Protection of Technologies Critical to U.S. National Security Interests
- Revamping Federal Oversight of Food Safety
- Protecting Public Health through Enhanced Oversight of Medical Products
- Transforming EPA's Processes for Assessing and Controlling Toxic Chemicals

Managing Federal Contracting More Effectively
- DOD Contract Management
- DOE's Contract Management for the National Nuclear Security Administration and Office of Environmental Management
- NASA Acquisition Management

Assessing the Efficiency and Effectiveness of Tax Law Administration
- Enforcement of Tax Laws

Modernizing and Safeguarding Insurance and Benefit Programs
- Improving and Modernizing Federal Disability Programs
- Pension Benefit Guaranty Corporation Insurance Programs
- Medicare Program
- Medicaid Program
- National Flood Insurance Program

Source: GAO

Mr. Chairman, Ranking Member Coburn, and Members of the Committee:

Thank you for the opportunity to discuss our 2013 government-wide high risk update[1] and to focus especially on the progress made in one high-risk area—*Strengthening Department of Homeland Security Management Functions*. Since 1990, we have regularly reported on government operations that we identified as high risk due to their greater vulnerability to fraud, waste, abuse, and mismanagement, or the need for transformation to address economy, efficiency, or effectiveness challenges. Our high risk program, supported by this committee and the House Committee on Oversight and Government Reform, has brought much-needed focus to problems impeding effective government and costing billions of dollars each year.

In November 2000, we published our criteria and process of determining those areas across government deemed to be high risk.[2] That document, based on input we received from Congress and the executive branch, including heads of major agencies and the Chief Financial Officers Council, specified that to determine which federal government programs and functions should be added to GAO's High Risk List, we consider whether the program or function is of national significance or is key to government performance and accountability. Further, we consider qualitative factors, such as whether the risk

- involves public health or safety, service delivery, national security, national defense, economic growth, or privacy or citizens' rights, or

- could result in significantly impaired service, program failure, injury or loss of life, or significantly reduced economy, efficiency, or effectiveness.

In addition, we also review the exposure to loss in quantitative terms, such as the value of major assets being impaired; revenue sources not being realized; or major agency assets being lost, stolen, damaged, or wasted. We also consider corrective measures planned or under way to

---

[1] GAO, *High-Risk Series: An Update*, GAO-13-283 (Washington, D.C.: February 2013).

[2] GAO, *Determining Performance and Accountability Challenges and High Risks*, GAO-01-159SP (Washington, D.C.: November 2000).

resolve a material control weakness and the status and effectiveness of these actions.

When legislative, administration, and agency actions, including those in response to our recommendations, result in significant progress toward resolving a high-risk problem, we remove the high-risk designation. As detailed in our November 2000 guidance, the five criteria for determining if a high-risk designation can be removed are:

- A demonstrated strong commitment and top leadership support to address the risk(s).

- The capacity (i.e., the people and other resources) to resolve the risk(s).

- A corrective action plan(s) that defines the root causes, identifies effective solutions, and provides for substantially completing corrective measures near term, including but not limited to steps necessary to implement solutions we recommended.

- A program instituted to monitor and independently validate the effectiveness and sustainability of corrective measures.

- The ability to demonstrate progress in having implemented corrective measures.

In recent years, Congress has passed several laws—which are discussed in our 2013 high risk update—targeting high-risk areas. In addition, top administration officials have continued to show their commitment to ensuring that high-risk areas receive attention and oversight. The Office of Management and Budget (OMB) regularly convenes meetings for agencies to provide progress updates on high-risk issues. When a high-risk issue area ranges across agencies, OMB coordinates with representatives from multiple agencies to participate. These meetings typically include OMB's Deputy Director for Management, top leadership from the agencies, other administration and agency staff members responsible for addressing the high-risk issue, as well as myself and others from GAO.

This congressional and agency commitment is critical to resolving high-risk issues. For example, the Department of Homeland Security (DHS) has made considerable progress in transforming its original component agencies into a single cabinet-level department and positioning itself to ultimately achieve its full potential. As a result, we narrowed the scope of the high-risk area as reflected in the changed name from *Implementing and Transforming the Department of Homeland Security* to *Strengthening the Department of Homeland Security Management Functions*.

While there has been notable progress addressing the 30 high-risk issues that are currently on GAO's High Risk List, much remains to be done. Our 2013 high risk update report and website[3] provide details for each of these issues, describing the nature of the risks, what actions have been taken to address them, and what remains to be done to make further progress. The details in our report, along with successful implementation by agencies and continued oversight by Congress, can form a solid foundation for progress to address risks and improve programs and operations.

Government-wide 2013 High Risk Update

High-Risk Designation Removed

For our 2013 high risk update, we determined that two areas warranted removal from the High Risk List due to the progress that had been made—*Management of Interagency Contracting* and *IRS Business Systems Modernization*. Additional details for both areas can be found in Appendix I. A brief summary follows.

Management of Interagency Contracting

Interagency contracting—where one agency either places an order using another agency's contract or obtains contracting support services from another agency—can help streamline the procurement process, take advantage of unique expertise in a particular type of procurement, and achieve savings. While this method of contracting can save the government money and effort when properly managed, it also poses a variety of risks.

In 2005, we designated the management of interagency contracting as high risk due in part to unclear lines of accountability between customer

---

[3]GAO's High Risk website, http://www.gao.gov/highrisk/.

and assisting agencies and the potential for improper use, including out-of-scope work and noncompliance with competition requirements. We identified the continuing need for additional management controls and guidance and clearer definitions of roles and responsibilities as keys to addressing these issues. We also highlighted challenges agencies faced in fully realizing the benefits of interagency contracts, including the lack of data and the risk of potential duplication when new contracting vehicles are created. To address these issues, we identified the need for a policy framework and business case analysis requirements to support the creation of certain new contracts and improved data on existing interagency contracts.

As detailed in our 2013 high risk update report, we are removing the management of interagency contracting from the High Risk List based on: (1) continued progress made by agencies in addressing identified deficiencies, (2) establishment of additional management controls, (3) creation of a policy framework for establishing new interagency contracts, and (4) steps taken to address the need for better data on these contracts.

Specifically, most agencies have taken steps to implement and reinforce interagency contracting policies to address prior concerns about the improper use of these contracts. For example, we have noted improvements in procedures used in making purchases on behalf of the Department of Defense (DOD)—the largest user of interagency contracts. These included better defined roles and responsibilities and enhanced controls over funding procedures. Additionally, the DOD Inspector General has reported a significant decrease in problems with DOD procurements through other federal agencies in congressionally mandated reviews of interagency acquisitions. With respect to management controls, Federal Acquisition Regulation (FAR) provisions on interagency acquisitions were revised to require that agencies make a best procurement approach determination to justify the use of an interagency contract and prepare written interagency agreements outlining the roles and responsibilities of customer and assisting organizations.[4] As we recently reported, OMB analyzed reports from the 24 agencies that account for almost all contract spending government-

---

[4]FAR § 17.502-1. The interim FAR rule was issued in December 2010; the final rule was issued in February 2012.

wide and found that most had implemented management controls to reinforce the new FAR requirements and strengthen the management of interagency acquisitions. All 24 agencies also reported having oversight mechanisms to ensure their internal controls were operating properly.[5] In response to congressional direction[6] and our prior recommendation, OMB established a policy framework in September 2011 to govern the creation of new interagency contract vehicles.[7] The framework addresses concerns about potential duplication by requiring agencies to develop a thorough business case prior to establishing certain contract vehicles. Finally, in response to our recommendations, OMB and the General Services Administration have taken a number of steps to address the need for better data on interagency contract vehicles. These efforts should enhance both government-wide efforts to manage interagency contracts and agency efforts to conduct market research and negotiate better prices.

Importantly, congressional oversight sustained over several years has been vital in addressing the issues that led this area to be designated high risk. Removing the management of interagency contracting from the High Risk List does not mean that the federal government's use of these contracts is without challenges. But, we believe there are mechanisms in place that OMB and federal agencies can use to identify and address interagency contracting issues before they put the government at significant risk for waste, fraud, or abuse. We also will continue to monitor developments in this area.

IRS Business Systems Modernization

Internal Revenue Service (IRS) Business Systems Modernization (BSM) is a multi-billion dollar, highly complex effort that involves the development and delivery of a number of modernized tax administration and internal management systems as well as core infrastructure projects

---

[5]GAO, *Interagency Contracting: Agency Actions Address Key Management Challenges, but Additional Steps Needed to Ensure Consistent Implementation of Policy Changes,* GAO-13-133R (Washington, D.C.: January 2013). We also reported on DOD's implementation of the new FAR requirements and found that for almost all of the selected orders, DOD effectively delineated roles and responsibilities by completing interagency agreements as required.

[6]Pub. L. No. 110-417, § 865 (2008).

[7]OMB, Office of Federal Procurement Policy, *Development, Review, and Approval of Business Cases for Certain Interagency and Agency-Specific Acquisitions* (Washington, D.C.: Sept. 29, 2011).

that are intended to replace the agency's aging business and tax processing systems.

In 1995, we identified serious management and technical weaknesses in IRS's modernization program that jeopardized its successful completion. We recommended many actions to fix the problems, and added IRS's modernization to GAO's High Risk List. In 1995, we also added IRS's financial management to GAO's High Risk List, due to long-standing and pervasive problems that hampered the effective collection of revenues and precluded the preparation of auditable financial statements.[8] We combined the two issues into one high-risk area in 2005 since resolution of the most serious financial management problems depended largely on the success of the business systems modernization program. Throughout the years, Congress conducted oversight of the BSM program by, among other things, requiring that IRS submit annual expenditure plans that needed to meet certain conditions, including a review by GAO. Because of the significant progress made in addressing the high-risk area, starting in fiscal year 2012, Congress did not require the submission of an annual expenditure plan.

We are removing the BSM program from the High Risk List because of progress made in addressing significant weaknesses in information technology and financial management capabilities. IRS delivered the initial phase of its cornerstone tax processing project and began the daily processing and posting of individual taxpayer accounts in January 2012. This enhanced tax administration and improved service by enabling faster refunds for more taxpayers, allowing more timely account updates and faster issuance of taxpayer notices. IRS has improved its investment management and project oversight processes. IRS also took additional steps to strengthen its IT management capabilities. For example, in July 2011, we noted that IRS had in place close to 80 percent of the practices needed for an effective investment management process, including all of the practices needed for effective project oversight.[9] In October 2011, we also reported that IRS had embarked on an effort to improve its software development practices using the Carnegie Mellon University Software

---

[8]GAO, *High-Risk Series: An Overview*, HR-95-1 (Washington, D.C.: Feb. 1, 1995).

[9]GAO, *Investment Management: IRS Has a Strong Oversight Process But Needs to Improve How It Continues Funding Ongoing Investments*, GAO-11-587 (Washington, D.C.: July 20, 2011).

Engineering Institute's Capability Maturity Model Integration (CMMI), which calls for disciplined software development and acquisition practices which are considered industry best practices. In September 2012, IRS's application development organization reached CMMI maturity level 3, a high achievement by industry standards.[10]

As with all areas removed from the High Risk List, we will continue to monitor how future events unfold both with the IRS modernization efforts and in the *Enforcement of Tax Laws*, which remains on the High Risk List.

New High-Risk Areas

This year, we added two new areas to the High Risk List—*Limiting the Federal Government's Fiscal Exposure by Better Managing Climate Change Risks* and *Mitigating Gaps in Weather Satellite Data*. Additional details for both areas can be found in Appendix II. A brief summary follows.

Limiting the Federal Government's Fiscal Exposure by Better Managing Climate Change Risks

Climate change is a complex, crosscutting issue that poses risks to many environmental and economic systems—including agriculture, infrastructure, ecosystems, and human health—and presents a significant financial risk to the federal government. Among other impacts, climate change could threaten coastal areas with rising sea levels, alter agricultural productivity, and increase the intensity and frequency of severe weather events. As observed by the United States Global Change Research Program, the impacts and costliness of weather disasters—resulting from floods, drought, and other events such as tropical cyclones—are expected to increase in significance as what are considered "rare" events become more common and intense due to anticipated changes in the global climate system. Moreover, according to the National Oceanic and Atmospheric Administration's National Climatic Data Center (NCDC), the United States has sustained 144 weather and climate-related disasters since 1980, in which overall damages reached

---

[10]The CMMI ranks organizational maturity according to five levels. Maturity levels 2 through 5 require verifiable existence and use of certain key process areas. At maturity level 3, known as the "defined" level, processes are well characterized and understood, and are described in standards, procedures, tools, and methods. The organization's set of standard processes, which is the basis for maturity level 3, is established and improved over time. A defined process clearly states the purpose, inputs, entry criteria, activities, roles, measures, verification steps, outputs, and exit criteria. In addition, processes are managed more proactively using an understanding of the interrelationships of process activities and detailed measures of the process, its work products, and its services.

or exceeded $1 billion each, with 14 events in 2011 and 11 events in 2012. NCDC estimates that 2012 will surpass 2011 in terms of aggregate costs for annual billion-dollar disasters, even with fewer disasters.

The federal government owns extensive infrastructure, such as defense installations, and manages 29 percent of the land in the United States; and insures property through the National Flood Insurance Program and crops through the Federal Crop Insurance Corporation. As of November 2012, FEMA owes the Treasury approximately $20 billion—up from $17.8 billion pre-Superstorm Sandy—and had not repaid any principal on the loan since 2010. Further, the federal government's crop insurance costs have increased in recent years—rising from an average of $3.1 billion per year from fiscal years 2000 through 2006, to an average of $7.6 billion per year from fiscal years 2007 through 2012—and ,according to the Congressional Budget Office, are projected to increase further.

The federal government also provides emergency aid in response to natural disasters. For example, we reported in September 2012 that major disaster declarations have increased over recent decades to a record of 98 in fiscal year 2011 compared with 65 in 2004. Had FEMA adjusted the indicator on which it principally relies to determine whether to recommend that a jurisdiction receive public assistance funding, to reflect changes in personal income and inflation, 44 percent and 25 percent fewer disaster declarations, respectively, would have met the threshold for public assistance during fiscal years 2004 through 2011. Over that period, the Federal Emergency Management Agency (FEMA) obligated more than $80 billion in federal assistance for major disasters.[11] The federal government's exposure to major disasters continues to pose risks. Most recently, Congress provided more than $60 billion in budget authority for disaster assistance in the wake of Superstorm Sandy.[12]

We have found that the federal government is not well positioned to address the fiscal exposure presented by climate change, and needs a government-wide strategic approach with strong leadership to manage

[11]GAO, *Federal Disaster Assistance: Improved Criteria Needed to Assess a Jurisdiction's Capability to Respond and Recover on Its Own*, GAO-12-838 (Washington, D.C.: Sept. 12, 2012).

[12]Congress provided $9.7 billion in borrowing authority for the National Flood Insurance Program and about $50.6 billion in appropriated funds. Pub. L. No. 113-1 (2013); Pub. L. No. 113-2 (2013).

related risks. We reported in 2009 that while policymakers increasingly viewed climate change adaptation—defined as adjustments to natural or human systems in response to actual or expected climate change—as a risk-management strategy to protect vulnerable sectors and communities that might be affected by changes in the climate, the federal government's emerging adaptation activities were carried out in an ad hoc manner and were not well coordinated across federal agencies, let alone with state and local governments.[13] Subsequently, in May 2011, we reported that there was no coherent strategic government-wide approach to climate change funding and that federal officials do not have a shared understanding of strategic government-wide priorities.[14] At that time, we recommended that the appropriate entities within the Executive Office of the President clearly establish federal strategic climate change priorities, including the roles and responsibilities of the key federal entities, taking into consideration the full range of climate-related activities within the federal government. The relevant federal entities have not directly addressed this recommendation.

Federal agencies have made some progress toward better organizing across agencies, within agencies, and among different levels of government; however, the increasing fiscal exposure for the federal government calls for more comprehensive and systematic strategic planning, including, but not limited to, the following:

- A government-wide strategic approach with strong leadership and the authority to manage climate change risks that encompasses the entire range of related federal activities and addresses all key elements of strategic planning. Federal agencies recently released draft climate change adaptation plans. While individual agency actions are necessary, a centralized strategy driven by a government-wide plan is also needed to reduce the federal fiscal exposure to climate change, maximize investments, achieve efficiencies, and better position the government for success.

---

[13]GAO, *Climate Change Adaptation: Strategic Federal Planning Could Help Government Officials Make More Informed Decisions*, GAO-10-113 (Washington, D.C.: Oct 7, 2009).

[14]GAO, *Climate Change: Improvements Needed to Clarify National Priorities and Better Align Them with Federal Funding Decisions*, GAO-11-317 (Washington, D.C.: May 20, 2011).

- More information to understand and manage federal insurance programs' long-term exposure to climate change and analyze the potential impacts of an increase in the frequency or severity of weather-related events on their operations.

- A government-wide approach for providing (1) the best available climate-related data for making decisions at the state and local level and (2) assistance for translating available climate-related data into information that officials need to make decisions.

- Potential gaps in satellite data need to be effectively addressed.

- Improved criteria for assessing a jurisdiction's capability to respond to and recover from a disaster without federal assistance, and to better apply lessons from past experience when developing disaster cost estimates.

Mitigating Gaps in Weather Satellite Data

Potential gaps in environmental satellite data beginning as early as 2014 and lasting as long as 53 months have led to concerns that future weather forecasts and warnings—including warnings of extreme events such as hurricanes, storm surges, and floods—will be less accurate and timely. A number of decisions are needed to ensure contingency and continuity plans can be implemented effectively. We and others—including an independent review team reporting to the Department of Commerce and the department's Inspector General—have raised concerns that problems and delays on environmental satellite acquisition programs will result in gaps in the continuity of critical satellite data used in weather forecasts and warnings. The importance of such data was recently highlighted by the advance warnings of the path, timing, and intensity of Superstorm Sandy.

Since the 1960s, the United States has used both polar-orbiting and geostationary satellites to observe the earth and its land, oceans, atmosphere, and space environments. Polar-orbiting satellites constantly circle the earth in an almost north-south orbit providing global coverage of environmental conditions that affect the weather and climate. As the earth rotates beneath it, each polar-orbiting satellite views the entire earth's surface twice a day. In contrast, geostationary satellites maintain a fixed position relative to the earth from a high-level orbit of about 22,300 miles in space. Used in combination with ground, sea, and airborne observing systems, both types of satellites have become an indispensable part of monitoring and forecasting weather and climate. Polar-orbiting satellites provide the data that go into numerical weather prediction models, which are a primary tool for forecasting weather days in advance—including forecasting the path and intensity of hurricanes and tropical storms. Geostationary satellites provide frequently-updated graphical images that are used to identify current weather patterns and provide short-term warnings.

In regards to polar satellites, the National Oceanic and Atmospheric Administration (NOAA) must make decisions about (1) whether and how to extend support for legacy satellite systems so that their data might be available if needed, (2) how much time and resources to invest in improving satellite models so that they assimilate data from alternative sources, (3) whether to pursue international agreements for access to additional satellite systems and how best to resolve any security issues with the foreign data, (4) when and how to test the value and integration of alternative data sources, and (5) how these preliminary mitigation plans will be integrated with NOAA's broader end-to-end plans for sustaining weather forecasting capabilities. NOAA must also identify time frames for when these decisions will be made. We have ongoing work assessing NOAA's efforts to limit and mitigate potential polar satellite data gaps.

For the geostationary satellites, NOAA must demonstrate its progress in conducting training and simulations for contingency scenarios, evaluating the status of viable foreign satellites, and working with the user community to account for differences in product coverage under contingency scenarios. These steps are critical for NOAA to move forward in documenting the processes it will take to implement its contingency plans. Once these activities are completed, NOAA should update its contingency plan to provide more details on its contingency scenarios, associated time frames, and any preventative actions it is taking to minimize the possibility of a gap. We have ongoing work assessing NOAA's actions to ensure that its plans are viable and that continuity procedures are in place and have been tested.

Modified High-Risk Area

One area—*Modernizing the Outdated U.S. Financial Regulatory System*—has been modified due to changing circumstances to include the Federal Housing Administration (FHA). To reflect these changing circumstances, the name of the area has been changed to *Modernizing the U.S. Financial Regulatory System and Federal Role in Housing Finance*. We first designated this area as high risk in 2009 due to the urgent need to reform the fragmented and outdated U.S. financial regulatory system. As detailed in our 2013 high risk update report, many actions are under way to implement oversight by new regulatory bodies and new requirements for market participants, although many rulemakings remain unfinished. Among the additional actions needed are resolving the role of the two housing-related government-sponsored enterprises—Fannie Mae and Freddie Mac—that continue operating under government conservatorships. However, a new challenge for the markets has also evolved as the decline in private sector participation in housing finance that began with the 2007-2009 financial crisis has resulted in much greater activity by FHA, whose single-family loan insurance portfolio has grown from about $300 billion in 2007 to more than $1.1 trillion in 2012. Although required to maintain capital reserves equal to at least 2 percent of its portfolio, FHA's capital reserves have fallen below this level, due partly to increases in projected defaults on the loans it has insured.

As a result, we are modifying this high-risk area to include FHA and acknowledging the need for actions beyond those already taken to help restore FHA's financial soundness and define its future role. One such action would be to determine the economic conditions that FHA's primary insurance fund would be expected to withstand without drawing on the Treasury. Recent events suggest that the 2-percent capital requirement may not be adequate to avoid the need for Treasury support under severe stress scenarios. Additionally, actions to reform the government-sponsored enterprises and to implement mortgage market reforms in the Dodd-Frank Act will need to consider the potential impacts on FHA's risk exposure.

Additional information on this area is provided on page 81 of our 2013 high risk update. [15]

---

[15] GAO-13-283.

Strengthening Department of Homeland Security Management Functions

Since our 2011 update, sufficient progress has been made to narrow the scope of three areas, including *Strengthening Department of Homeland Security Management Functions*.[16] In 2003, we designated implementing and transforming the Department of Homeland Security (DHS) as high risk because DHS had to transform 22 agencies—several with major management challenges—into one department. Further, failure to effectively address DHS's management and mission risks could have serious consequences for U.S. national and economic security. Given the significant effort required to build and integrate a department as large and complex as DHS, our initial high-risk designation addressed the department's initial transformation and subsequent implementation efforts, to include associated management and programmatic challenges. At that time, we reported that the creation of DHS was an enormous undertaking that would take time to achieve, and that the successful transformation of large organizations, even those undertaking less strenuous reorganizations, could take years to implement.

Over the past 10 years, the focus of this high-risk area has evolved in tandem with DHS's maturation and evolution. The overriding tenet has consistently remained the department's ability to build a single, cohesive and effective department that is greater than the sum of its parts—a goal that requires effective collaboration and integration of its various components and management functions. In 2007, in reporting on DHS's progress since its creation, as well as in our 2009 high risk update, we reported that DHS had made more progress in implementing its range of missions rather than its management functions, and that continued work was needed to address an array of programmatic and management challenges.

DHS's initial focus on mission implementation was understandable given the critical homeland security needs facing the nation after the department's establishment, and the challenges posed by its creation, integration and transformation. As DHS continued to mature, and as we reported in our assessment of DHS's progress and challenges 10 years after 9/11, we found that the department implemented key homeland security operations and achieved important goals in many areas to create

---

[16]*Federal Oil and Gas Resources and Department of Energy's Contract Management for the National Nuclear Security Administration and Office of Environmental Management* were the other high-risk areas that were narrowed. Appendix III has information on these issues.

and strengthen a foundation to reach its potential.[17] However, we also identified that more work remained for DHS to address weaknesses in its operational and implementation efforts, and to strengthen the efficiency and effectiveness of those efforts. We further reported that continuing weaknesses in DHS's management functions had been a key theme impacting the department's implementation efforts. Recognizing DHS's progress in transformation and mission implementation, our 2011 high risk update focused on the continued need to strengthen DHS's management functions (acquisition, information technology, financial management, and human capital) and integrate those functions within and across the department, as well as the impact of these challenges on the department's ability to effectively and efficiently carry out its missions.

While challenges remain for DHS to address across its range of missions, the department has made considerable progress in transforming its original component agencies into a single cabinet-level department and positioning itself to achieve its full potential. As a result, we narrowed the scope of the high-risk area and changed the name from Implementing and Transforming the Department of Homeland Security to Strengthening the Department of Homeland Security Management Functions.

Since our last high risk update in January 2011, we have regularly met with senior DHS officials to discuss the department's progress in addressing this high-risk area and written letters summarizing our feedback on DHS's progress and work remaining to address the high-risk designation, most recently in December 2012. Our ongoing dialogue with DHS at the most senior levels has enabled us to understand DHS's perspectives and provided an opportunity for us to consistently communicate our views on DHS's progress and work remaining. DHS has made important progress in implementing, transforming, strengthening, and integrating its management functions, including taking numerous

---

[17]GAO, *Department of Homeland Security: Progress Made and Work Remaining in Implementing Homeland Security Missions 10 Years after 9/11*, GAO-11-881 (Washington, D.C.: Sept. 7, 2011). This report addressed DHS's progress in implementing its homeland security missions since it began operations, work remaining, and issues affecting implementation efforts. Drawing from more than 1,000 GAO reports and congressional testimony issued related to DHS programs and operations, and approximately 1,500 recommendations made to strengthen mission and management implementation, this report addressed progress and remaining challenges in such areas as border security and immigration, transportation security, and emergency management, among others.

actions specifically designed to address our criteria for removing areas from the High Risk List; however, this area remains high risk because the department has significant work ahead.

Leadership commitment. The Secretary, Deputy Secretary, and Under Secretary for Management of Homeland Security and other senior officials have continued to demonstrate commitment and top leadership support for addressing the department's management challenges. They have also taken actions to institutionalize this commitment to help ensure the long-term success of the department's efforts. For example, in May 2012, the Secretary of Homeland Security modified the delegations of authority between the Management Directorate and its counterparts at the component level to clarify and strengthen the authorities of the Under Secretary for Management across the department. Senior DHS officials have also periodically met with us over the past 4 years to discuss the department's plans and progress in addressing this high-risk area, during which we provided feedback on the department's efforts. According to these officials, and as demonstrated through their progress, the department is committed to demonstrating measurable, sustained progress in addressing this high-risk area.

Corrective action plan. DHS has established a plan for addressing this high-risk area. Specifically, in a September 2010 letter to DHS, we identified and DHS agreed to achieve 31 actions and outcomes that are critical to addressing the challenges within the department's management areas and in integrating those functions across the department. These key actions and outcomes include, among others, validating required acquisition documents in accordance with a department-approved, knowledge-based acquisition process, and obtaining and then sustaining unqualified audit opinions for at least 2 consecutive years on the department-wide financial statements. In January 2011, DHS issued its initial Integrated Strategy for High Risk Management, which included key management initiatives and related corrective action plans for addressing its management challenges and the outcomes we identified. DHS provided updates of its progress in implementing these initiatives and corrective actions in its later versions of the strategy—June 2011, December 2011, June 2012, and September 2012. The comprehensive strategy, if implemented and sustained, provides a path for DHS to be removed from GAO's High Risk List.

Framework to monitor progress. DHS has established a framework for monitoring its progress in implementing its corrective actions and addressing the 31 actions and outcomes. In the June 2012 update to the

Integrated Strategy for High Risk Management, DHS included, for the first time, performance measures to track its progress in implementing all of its key management initiatives. Additionally, the Under Secretary for Management holds quarterly internal progress review meetings with senior officials from each management function to discuss progress toward achieving milestones and meeting performance goals. It will be important for DHS to continue to track progress toward achieving its goals and monitor and refine its measures and corrective actions, as needed.

Capacity. In June 2012, DHS identified the resources needed to implement most (154 of 173) of its corrective actions, but needs to continue to identify resources for the remaining corrective actions; determine that sufficient resources and staff are committed to initiatives; work to mitigate shortfalls and prioritize initiatives, as needed; and communicate to senior leadership critical resource gaps. DHS also identified ways in which it is leveraging resources to implement corrective actions, which is particularly important in light of constrained budgets. For example, in October 2012, DHS reported that it is pooling resources and working across functional lines to create cross functional, matrixed teams and executive steering committees to ensure timely implementation of the strategy. However, it is too soon to determine whether this approach is a sustainable way for DHS to address the resource challenges and capacity gaps that have affected its implementation efforts at the department and component levels.

Demonstrated, sustained progress. DHS has made important progress in implementing corrective actions across its management functions, but it has not yet demonstrated sustainable, measurable progress in addressing key challenges that continue to remain within these functions and in the integration of those functions. DHS has implemented a number of actions demonstrating the department's progress in improving its management functions. For example, DHS established the Office of Program Accountability and Risk Management in October 2011 to be responsible for the department's overall acquisition governance process. DHS also established a formal IT Program Management Development Track and staffed Centers of Excellence with subject matter experts to that as of March 2012, approximately two-thirds of the department's major IT investments we reviewed (47 of 68) were meeting current cost and schedule commitments (i.e., goals). Additionally, in the financial management area, DHS has reduced the number of material weaknesses in internal controls and obtained a qualified audit opinion on its fiscal year 2012 financial statements. DHS has also implemented common policies, procedures, and systems, such as those related to human capital, across its management functions.

However, DHS still has considerable work ahead in many areas. For example, in September 2012, we reported that most of DHS's major acquisition programs continue to cost more than expected, take longer to deploy than planned, or deliver less capability than promised. We identified 42 programs that experienced cost growth or schedule slips, or both, with 16 of the programs' costs increasing from a total of $19.7 billion in 2008 to $52.2 billion in 2011—an aggregate increase of 166 percent. Further, while DHS has defined and begun to implement a vision for a tiered governance structure to improve information technology (IT) management, we reported in July 2012 that the governance structure covers less than 20 percent (about 16 of 80) of DHS's major IT investments and 3 of its 13 portfolios. DHS has also been unable to obtain an audit opinion on its internal controls over financial reporting, and needs to obtain and sustain unqualified audit opinions for at least two consecutive years on the department-wide financial statements. Finally, federal surveys have consistently found that DHS employees are less satisfied with their jobs than the government-wide average. Key to addressing the department's management challenges is DHS demonstrating the ability to achieve sustained progress across the 31 actions and outcomes we identified as needed to address the high-risk designation, to which DHS agreed. As shown in table 1, we believe DHS has fully addressed 6, mostly addressed 2, partially addressed 16, and initiated 7 of the 31 key actions and outcomes.

Table 1: Assessment of DHS's Progress in Addressing Key Actions and Outcomes

Key outcomes	Fully addressed[a]	Mostly addressed[b]	Partially addressed[c]	Initiated[d]	Total
Acquisition management			2	3	5
IT management	1	1	4		6
Financial management	2		3	4	9
Human capital management		1	6		7
Management integration	3		1		4
Total	6	2	16	7	31

Source: GAO analysis of DHS documents, interviews, and prior GAO reports.

[a]"Fully Addressed": Outcome is fully addressed.

[b]"Mostly Addressed": Progress is significant and a small amount of work remains.

[c]"Partially Addressed": Progress is measurable, but significant work remains.

[d]"Initiated": Activities have been initiated to address outcome, but it is too early to report progress.

To more fully address our high-risk designation, DHS needs to continue implementing its *Integrated Strategy for High Risk Management* and show measurable, sustainable progress in implementing its key management initiatives and corrective actions and achieving outcomes. In doing so, it will be important for DHS to:

- make continued progress in addressing the 31 actions and outcomes and demonstrate that systems, personnel, and policies are in place to ensure that progress can be sustained over time;

- maintain its current level of top leadership support and sustained commitment to ensure continued progress in executing its corrective actions through completion;

- continue to implement its plan for addressing this high-risk area and periodically report its progress to Congress and GAO;

- closely track and independently validate the effectiveness and sustainability of its corrective actions and make midcourse adjustments, as needed; and

- monitor the effectiveness of its efforts to establish reliable resource estimates at the department and component levels, address and work to mitigate any resource gaps, and prioritize initiatives as needed to ensure it has the capacity to implement and sustain its corrective actions.

We will continue to monitor DHS's efforts in this high-risk area to determine if the actions and outcomes are achieved and sustained.

Additional information on this area is provided on page 161 of our 2013 high risk update.[18]

Sustaining Attention on High-Risk Programs

Overall, the government continues to take high-risk problems seriously and is making long-needed progress toward correcting them. Congress has acted to address several individual high-risk areas through hearings and legislation. Our high risk update and high risk website, http://www.gao.gov/highrisk/, can help inform the oversight agenda for the 113th Congress and guide efforts of the administration and agencies to improve government performance and reduce waste and risks. In support of Congress and to further progress to address high-risk issues, we continue to review efforts and make recommendations to address high-risk areas problems. Continued perseverance in addressing high-risk areas will ultimately yield significant benefits.

In that regard, the Government Performance Results Act (GPRA) Modernization Act of 2010 (GPRAMA) provides the Executive Branch and Congress with new tools to identify and address management weaknesses that are undermining agencies' capacity to achieve results. For example, the act requires agencies, in their annual performance plans, to describe the major management challenges they face—which, by definition, cover issues we have identified as high risk—as well as the actions they plan to address these challenges. In addition, agencies are to identify performance goals, performance measures, and milestones to gauge progress toward resolving these challenges.

In addition, OMB is required to develop long-term goals to improve management functions across the government. The act specifies that these goals should include five areas: financial management, human capital management, information technology management, procurement

---

[18]GAO-13-283.

and acquisition management, and real property management. We have identified these areas as key management challenges for the government. Moreover, some aspects of these areas have warranted our designation as high risk, either government-wide or at certain agencies. OMB is required to provide clear milestones and periodic status reports on progress being made and actions needed for additional progress.

Over the years, the Committee on Homeland Security and Governmental Affairs and its predecessors have done commendable work focusing attention on improving government management and performance—by reporting out legislation, such as the original GPRA and GPRAMA, and through hearings, such as this one. Moving forward, congressional oversight and sustained attention by top administration officials will be essential to ensure further improvement in the management and performance of federal programs and operations and addressing high-risk areas.

Thank you, Mr. Chairman, Ranking Member Coburn, and Members of the Committee. This concludes my testimony. I would be pleased to answer questions.

For further information on GAO's high risk program, contact J. Christopher Mihm at (202) 512-6806 or mihmj@gao.gov. For information on DHS, contact Cathleen A. Berrick, 202-512-3404 or berrickc@gao.gov. Contact points for the individual high-risk areas are listed in GAO-13-283 and on our high-risk website, http://www.gao.gov/highrisk. Contact points for our Congressional Relations and Public Affairs offices may be found on the last page of this statement.

Appendix I: High-Risk Designation Removed

Management of Interagency Contracting

We are removing the management of interagency contracting from the High Risk List based on (1) continued progress made by agencies in addressing previously identified deficiencies, (2) establishment of additional management controls, (3) creation of a policy framework for establishing new interagency contracts, and (4) steps taken to address the need for better data on these contracts. Congressional oversight and the leadership of the Office of Management and Budget's (OMB) Office of Federal Procurement Policy (OFPP)—which provides direction on government-wide procurement policies—have been vital in addressing the issues that led this area to be designated high risk.

Interagency contracting—where one agency either places an order using another agency's contract or obtains contracting support services from another agency—can help streamline the procurement process, take advantage of unique expertise in a particular type of procurement, and achieve savings. Interagency contracts are designed to leverage the government's buying power and allow for agencies to meet the demands for goods and services at a time when the federal government is focused on achieving efficiencies in the acquisition process. While this method of contracting can save the government money and effort when properly managed, it also poses a variety of risks.

In 2005, we designated the management of interagency contracting as high risk due in part to unclear lines of accountability between customer and assisting agencies and the potential for improper use, including out-of-scope work and noncompliance with competition requirements.[1] In our 2007 high risk update, we identified the continuing need for (1) additional management controls and guidance and (2) clearer definitions of roles and responsibilities as the keys to addressing these issues.[2] In our 2011 high risk update, we highlighted additional challenges agencies faced in fully realizing the benefits of interagency contracts, including the lack of data and the risk of potential duplication when new contracting vehicles are created.[3] Duplication among interagency contracts can result in missed opportunities to leverage the government's buying power and may adversely affect the administrative efficiencies and cost savings expected

---

[1]GAO, *High-Risk Series: An Update*, GAO-05-207 (Washington, D.C.: January 2005).

[2]GAO, *High-Risk Series: An Update*, GAO-07-310 (Washington, D.C.: January 2007).

[3]GAO, *High-Risk Series: An Update*, GAO-11-278 (Washington, D.C.: February 2011).

GAO-13-444T

with their use. To address these issues, our prior work identified the need for (1) a policy framework and business case analysis requirements to support the creation of certain new contracts and (2) improved data on existing interagency contracts.

The federal government has made significant progress in reducing the interagency contracting risks that led to our high-risk designation. In our 2009 and 2011 high risk updates we noted improvements in procedures used in making purchases on behalf of the Department of Defense (DOD)—the largest user of interagency contracts. These included better defined roles and responsibilities and enhanced controls over funding procedures. Additionally, the DOD Inspector General has reported a significant decrease in problems with DOD procurements through other federal agencies in congressionally mandated reviews of interagency acquisitions. We also noted that the General Services Administration (GSA) and OMB have established corrective action plans to implement our prior recommendations. Since our last update, as discussed in the following sections, federal agencies have continued to address weaknesses related to the use, creation, and oversight of interagency contracting vehicles.

Strengthened management controls for the use of interagency contracts. Most agencies have taken steps to implement and reinforce interagency contracting policies to address prior concerns about the improper use of these contracts. In response to congressional direction,[4] Federal Acquisition Regulation (FAR) provisions on interagency acquisitions were revised to require that agencies make a best procurement approach determination to justify the use of an interagency contract and prepare written interagency agreements outlining the roles and responsibilities of customer and assisting organizations.[5] The best procurement approach determination ensures that the requesting agency considers factors such as the suitability of the contract vehicle and compliance with laws and policies. Congress also strengthened requirements for interagency acquisitions performed on behalf of DOD as well as the competition rules for placing orders on multiple-award

---

[4]Pub. L. No. 110-417, § 865 (2008).

[5]FAR § 17.502-1. The interim FAR rule was issued in December 2010; the final rule was issued in February 2012.

contracts, which are commonly used in interagency acquisitions.[5] As we recently reported, OMB's October 2012 analysis of reports from the 24 agencies that account for almost all contract spending government-wide found that most had implemented management controls to reinforce the new FAR requirements and strengthen the management of interagency acquisitions. All 24 agencies also reported having oversight mechanisms to ensure their internal controls were operating properly.[7]

New controls over creation of new interagency contract vehicles. In response to congressional direction[8] and our prior recommendation, OMB established a policy framework in September 2011 to govern the creation of new interagency contract vehicles.[9] The framework addresses concerns about potential duplication by requiring agencies to develop a thorough business case prior to establishing certain contract vehicles. The guidance further requires senior agency officials to approve the business cases and post them on an OMB website to provide interested federal stakeholders an opportunity to offer feedback. OMB then is able to conduct follow-up with sponsoring agencies if significant questions, including ones related to duplication, are raised during the vetting process. OMB also has established a new strategic sourcing governance council, which is expected to examine how to use existing interagency contract vehicles to support government-wide strategic sourcing efforts.

Improved data on interagency contracts. In response to our recommendations, OMB and GSA have taken a number of steps to address the need for better data on interagency contract vehicles. These efforts should enhance both government-wide efforts to manage interagency contracts and agency efforts to conduct market research and negotiate better prices. To promote better and easier access to data on

---

[5]Pub. L. No. 110-181, § 801(b) (2008) and Pub. L. No. 110-417, § 863 (2008).

[7]GAO, *Interagency Contracting: Agency Actions Address Key Management Challenges, but Additional Steps Needed to Ensure Consistent Implementation of Policy Changes,* GAO-13-133R (Washington, D.C.: January 2013). We also reported on DOD's implementation of the new FAR requirements and found that for almost all of the selected orders, DOD effectively delineated roles and responsibilities by completing interagency agreements as required.

[8]Pub. L. No. 110-417, § 865 (2008).

[9]OMB, OFPP, *Development, Review, and Approval of Business Cases for Certain Interagency and Agency-Specific Acquisitions* (Washington, D.C.: Sept. 29, 2011).

existing contracts, OMB has made improvements to its Interagency Contract Directory, a searchable online database of indefinite-delivery vehicles available for interagency use. It has also posted information on government-wide acquisition contracts and blanket purchase agreements available for use under the Federal Strategic Sourcing Initiative on an OMB website, accessible by federal agencies.[10] Improving the availability of data is also a key facet of GSA's Schedules Modernization initiative, launched in June 2012. GSA has several pilot projects underway to collect and share data on its Multiple Award Schedules program, with the goal of improving pricing. GSA also has assembled a data team to improve access to comprehensive and reliable data across GSA contracting programs.

Removing the management of interagency contracting from the High Risk List does not mean that the federal government's use of these contracts is without challenges. For example, we and the DOD Inspector General have found instances in which DOD did not complete best procurement approach determinations as required.[11] Continued management attention is necessary. But, we believe there are mechanisms in place that OMB and federal agencies can use to identify and address interagency contracting issues before they put the government at significant risk for waste, fraud, or abuse. For example, the revised FAR rules on interagency acquisitions require senior procurement executives to submit an annual report on interagency acquisitions to OMB, which can use these to identify issues and risks at the agency level as well as government-wide trends. In addition, many agencies have reported building interagency contracting into internal reviews. Finally, we plan to continue to monitor the management of interagency contracts in our reviews of federal contracting.

---

[10]The Federal Strategic Sourcing Initiative was established in 2005 to address government-wide opportunities to strategically source commonly purchased products and services.

[11]GAO-13-133R and Department of Defense, Inspector General, *Contracting Improvements Still Needed in DOD's FY 2011Purchases Made Through the Department of Veterans Affairs*, DODIG-2013-028 (Alexandria, VA.: Dec. 7, 2012).

IRS Business Systems Modernization

We are removing the Internal Revenue Service's (IRS) Business Systems Modernization (BSM) program from the High Risk List because of IRS's progress in addressing the significant weaknesses in information technology (IT) and financial management capabilities that led to the high-risk designation, and its commitment to sustaining progress in the future. As we have with other areas we have removed, we will continue to monitor this area, as appropriate, to ensure that the improvements we have noted are sustained.

BSM is a multi-billion dollar, highly-complex effort that involves the development and delivery of a number of modernized tax administration and internal management systems as well as core infrastructure projects that are intended to replace the agency's aging business and tax processing systems. It is critical to providing improved and expanded service to taxpayers and internal business efficiencies for IRS and providing the reliable and timely financial management information needed to better enable the agency to justify its resource allocation decisions and funding requests. IRS began modernizing its timeworn, paper-intensive approach to tax returns processing in the mid-1980s.

In 1995, we identified serious management and technical weaknesses in the modernization program that jeopardized its successful completion. We recommended many actions to fix the problems, and added IRS's modernization to our High Risk List. In 1995, we also added the agency's financial management to our High Risk List due to long-standing and pervasive problems which hampered the effective collection of revenues and precluded the preparation of auditable financial statements.[12] We combined the two issues into one high-risk area in 2005 since resolution of the most serious financial management problems depended largely on the success of the business systems modernization program.

In 2007 and 2009, we reported that IRS had made progress in establishing management capabilities and addressing financial management weaknesses.[13] For example, in 2007, the agency developed a high-level modernization vision and strategy to address program changes and provide a modernization road map. In addition, it developed

---

[12]GAO, High-Risk Series: An Overview, HR-95-1 (Washington, D.C.: Feb. 1, 1995).

[13]GAO, High-Risk Series: An Update, GAO-09-271 (Washington, D.C.: Jan. 22, 2009), and GAO-07-310.

policies, procedures, and tools for developing and managing project requirements. IRS also implemented the initial phase of several key automated financial management systems, including a cost accounting module that it populated with data; developed a methodology to allocate costs to its business units; improved the reliability of its property and equipment records; and made significant progress in addressing long-standing deficiencies in controls over tax revenue collections, tax refund disbursements, and hard-copy tax receipts and related data. In addition, IRS completed several pilot projects to demonstrate its ability to determine the full cost of its programs and activities.

However, we kept BSM on the High Risk List because many challenges remained, including (1) improving processes for delivering modernized IT systems within cost and schedule estimates, (2) developing the cost and revenue information needed to support day-to-day decision making, and (3) addressing outstanding weaknesses in information security.[14] Throughout those years, Congress conducted oversight of the BSM program by, among other things, requiring that IRS submit annual expenditure plans that needed to meet certain conditions, including a review by GAO.

In our 2011 high risk update,[15] we reported that IRS had continued to make progress in addressing weaknesses in response to our recommendations but needed to leverage its capabilities to successfully deliver its BSM projects. Specifically, we noted that IRS needed to successfully deliver the initial phase of the Customer Account Data Engine 2 (CADE 2)—its cornerstone tax processing project—by moving the processing of individual taxpayer accounts from a weekly processing cycle to a daily processing cycle and delivering a modernized individual taxpayer account database by 2012. We also noted that IRS needed to continue its efforts to achieve expected benefits, including faster refunds, improved customer service, and faster resolution of taxpayer account issues (phase 2 of CADE 2). For financial management issues, in addition to addressing outstanding recommendations, including those associated with information security controls affecting the reliability of financial data, we noted that IRS needed to (1) ensure corrective action plans address all issues and define root causes and (2) strengthen its program for

---

[14]GAO-09-271.

[15]GAO-11-278.

monitoring the effectiveness of corrective actions taken in response to our information security recommendations.

Since 2011, IRS has worked to address these issues. For example, the agency delivered the initial phase of CADE 2 and began the daily processing and posting of individual taxpayer accounts in January 2012, enhancing tax administration and improving service by enabling faster refunds for more taxpayers, allowing more timely account updates, and faster issuance of taxpayer notices. [16] Also, in March 2012, IRS established the database housing all individual taxpayer account data and has plans underway to gradually increase its use for customer service and compliance purposes. Further, in May 2012, IRS initiated plans for phase 2 of CADE 2, which is in large part intended to address the unpaid assessment financial material weakness we have reported on in the past. As IRS progresses with this planning effort, it will be important for the agency to identify functionality it can deliver early on so it can begin reaping benefits for its employees and taxpayers and making progress towards retiring the legacy Individual Master File.

IRS also made important progress in addressing information systems-related internal control deficiencies, particularly those involving its networks and systems that had reduced the overall effectiveness of its information security controls and therefore the reliability of its financial data. [17] Notable among these efforts were the (1) formation of cross functional working groups tasked with the identification and remediation of specific at-risk control areas, (2) improvement in controls over the encryption of data transferred between accounting systems, and (3) upgrades to critical network devices on the agency's internal network system. In addition, during fiscal year 2012, IRS continued to devote significant attention and resources to addressing information security controls, and resolved a significant number of the information system-related internal control deficiencies that we previously reported. For example, IRS (1) addressed its outdated operating system and

---

[16]According to IRS, during Filing Season 2012, CADE 2 allowed more timely account updates (taxpayer account updates are viewable by IRS customer service representatives within 48 hours versus an average of 9 days in Filing Season 2011), and faster issuance of taxpayer notices (2.7 million notices sent to taxpayers with accounts processed daily versus 284,000 in Filing Season 2011).

[17]GAO, *Financial Audit: IRS's Fiscal Years 2012 and 2011 Financial Statements,* GAO-13-120 (Washington, D.C.: Nov. 9, 2012).

application software so that the versions in use are now supported by vendors, (2) improved the auditing and monitoring capabilities of a general support system, and (3) tested its general ledger system for tax transactions in its current operating environment. Further, IRS funded critical software upgrades for some of its key financial reporting systems, including its administrative accounting system and its procurement system, which was an important step toward addressing its information system issues. These improvements led us to conclude that IRS's remaining deficiencies in internal controls over information security no longer constitute a material weakness for financial reporting as of September 30, 2012. However, IRS still needs to strengthen its program for monitoring the effectiveness of corrective actions taken in response to our information security recommendations.

IRS also took additional steps to strengthen its IT management capabilities. For example, in July 2011, we noted that IRS had in place close to 80 percent of the practices needed for an effective investment management process, including all of the practices needed for effective project oversight.[18] In October 2011, we also reported that IRS had embarked on an effort to improve its software development practices using the Carnegie Mellon University Software Engineering Institute's Capability Maturity Model Integration (CMMI), which calls for disciplined software development and acquisition practices which are considered industry best practices. In September 2012, IRS's application development organization reached CMMI maturity level 3, a high achievement by industry standards.[19]

Finally, in October 2011, we highlighted CADE 2 as one of seven successful acquisitions in the federal government because, up to that

---

[18]GAO, *Investment Management: IRS Has a Strong Oversight Process But Needs to Improve How It Continues Funding Ongoing Investments*, GAO-11-587 (Washington, D.C.: July 20, 2011).

[19]The CMMI ranks organizational maturity according to five levels. Maturity levels 2 through 5 require verifiable existence and use of certain key process areas. At maturity level 3, known as the "defined" level, processes are well characterized and understood, and are described in standards, procedures, tools, and methods. The organization's set of standard processes, which is the basis for maturity level 3, is established and improved over time. A defined process clearly states the purpose, inputs, entry criteria, activities, roles, measures, verification steps, outputs, and exit criteria. In addition, processes are managed more proactively using an understanding of the interrelationships of process activities and detailed measures of the process, its work products, and its services.

point, it had achieved cost, schedule, scope, and performance goals through the use of critical success factors, including program staff actively engaged with stakeholders. program staff having the right knowledge and skills, agency executives engaged in the program, and streamlined and targeted governance.[20],[21] IRS officials are also applying these critical success factors to other programs at IRS. Because of the significant progress made in addressing this high-risk area over the years, starting in fiscal year 2012, Congress did not require the submission of an annual expenditure plan.

While we are removing IRS's BSM program from the High Risk List, we will nonetheless continue to closely monitor the agency's efforts because the modernization program is complex and critical to administering and enforcing tax laws. In addition, the remaining recurring deficiencies in information security, along with new deficiencies we identified during our audit of IRS's fiscal year 2012 financial statements, merit continued and consistent commitment and attention from IRS management. Specifically, IRS will need to continue to take steps to (1) improve its testing and monitoring capabilities, (2) ensure that policies and procedures are updated, and (3) address unresolved and newly identified control deficiencies, to sustain progress in improving its information system controls and have greater assurance that financial and taxpayer data will not remain vulnerable to inappropriate use, modification, or disclosure, possibly without being detected. We currently have a mandate to perform annual reviews of IRS's major information technology programs and also perform the annual audit of IRS's annual financial statements including the effectiveness of internal controls over financial reporting systems. We plan to continue to monitor IRS's BSM program through these reviews.

---

[20]GAO, *Information Technology: Critical Factors Underlying Successful Major Acquisitions*, GAO-12-7 (Washington, D.C.: Oct. 21, 2011).

[21]In quarterly status briefings to us and the Senate and House of Representatives Appropriations Committees, IRS has been reporting that the first phase of the CADE 2 program is still generally on track.

Appendix II: New High-Risk Areas

Limiting the Federal Government's Fiscal Exposure by Better Managing Climate Change Risks

Climate change poses risks to many environmental and economic systems—including agriculture, infrastructure, ecosystems, and human health—and presents a significant financial risk to the federal government. The United States Global Change Research Program (USGCRP) has observed that the impacts and costliness of weather disasters will increase in significance as what are considered 'rare' events become more common and intense due to climate change.[1] Among other impacts, climate change could threaten coastal areas with rising sea levels, alter agricultural productivity, and increase the intensity and frequency of severe weather events such as floods, drought, and hurricanes. Weather-related events have cost the nation tens of billions of dollars in damages over the past decade. For example, in 2012, the administration requested $60.4 billion for Superstorm Sandy recovery efforts. These impacts pose significant financial risks for the federal government, which owns extensive infrastructure, insures property through federal flood and crop insurance programs, provides technical assistance to state and local governments, and provides emergency aid in response to natural disasters. However, the federal government is not well positioned to address this fiscal exposure, partly because of the complex, cross-cutting nature of the issue. Given these challenges and the nation's precarious fiscal condition, we have added *Limiting the Federal Government's Fiscal Exposure to Climate Change* to our 2013 list of high-risk areas.[2]

Climate change adaptation—defined as adjustments to natural or human systems in response to actual or expected climate change—is a risk-management strategy to help protect vulnerable sectors and communities that might be affected by changes in the climate. For example, adaptation measures may include raising river or coastal dikes to protect

---

[1]Thomas R. Karl, Jerry M. Melillo, and Thomas C. Peterson, eds. *Global Climate Change Impacts in the United States* (Cambridge University Press: 2009). USGCRP coordinates and integrates the activities of 13 federal agencies that conduct research on changes in the global environment and their implications for society. USGCRP began as a presidential initiative in 1989 and was codified in the Global Change Research Act of 1990 [Pub. L. No. 101-606, § 103 (1990)]. USGCRP-participating agencies are the Departments of Agriculture, Commerce, Defense, Energy, Interior, Health and Human Services, State, and Transportation; U.S. Agency for International Development; Environmental Protection Agency; National Aeronautics and Space Administration; the National Science Foundation; and the Smithsonian Institution.

[2]The focus of this high-risk area may evolve over time to the extent that federal climate change programs and policies change.

infrastructure from sea level rise, building higher bridges, and increasing the capacity of storm water systems. Policymakers increasingly view climate change adaptation as a risk-management strategy to protect vulnerable sectors and communities that might be affected by changes in the climate, but, as we reported in 2009, the federal government's emerging adaptation activities were carried out in an ad hoc manner and were not well coordinated across federal agencies, let alone with state and local governments.[3]

The federal government has a number of efforts underway to decrease domestic greenhouse gas emissions, but decreasing global emissions depends in large part on cooperative international efforts. Further, according to the National Research Council (NRC) and USGCRP, greenhouse gases already in the atmosphere will continue altering the climate system for many decades. As such, the impacts of climate change can be expected to increase fiscal exposure for the federal government in many areas:

- *Federal government as property owner*. The federal government owns and operates hundreds of thousands of buildings and facilities that could be affected by a changing climate. In addition, the federal government manages about 650 million acres—29 percent of the 2.27 billion acres of U.S. land—for a wide variety of purposes, such as recreation, grazing, timber, and fish and wildlife. In 2007, we recommended that that the Secretaries of Agriculture, Commerce, and the Interior develop guidance for resource managers that explains how they are expected to address the effects of climate changes, and the three departments generally agreed with the recommendation. We have ongoing work related to adapting infrastructure and the management of federal lands to a changing climate.

- *Federal insurance programs*. Two important federal insurance efforts—the National Flood Insurance Program (NFIP) and the Federal Crop Insurance Corporation—are based on conditions, priorities, and approaches that were established decades ago and do not account for climate change. NFIP has been on our High Risk List since March 2006 because of concerns about its long-term financial

---

[3]GAO, *Climate Change Adaptation: Strategic Federal Planning Could Help Government Officials Make More Informed Decisions*, GAO-10-113 (Washington, D.C.: Oct. 7, 2009).

solvency and related operational issues.[4] In March 2007, we reported that both of these insurance programs' exposure to weather-related losses had grown substantially, and that the agencies responsible for them had done little to develop the information necessary to understand their long-term exposure to climate change.[5] We recommended that the responsible agencies analyze the potential long-term fiscal implications of climate change and report their findings to Congress. The agencies agreed with the recommendation and contracted with experts to study their programs' long-term exposure to climate change, but the results of the work have not yet been reported to Congress. In addition, in June 2011, we reported that external factors continue to complicate the administration of NFIP and affect its financial stability.[6] In particular, the Federal Emergency Management Agency (FEMA), which administers NFIP, has not been authorized to account for long-term erosion when updating flood maps used to set premium rates for NFIP, increasing the likelihood that premiums would not cover future losses. We suggested that Congress consider authorizing NFIP to account for long-term flood erosion in its flood maps, and the Biggert-Waters Flood Insurance Reform Act of 2012 requires FEMA to use information on topography, coastal erosion areas, changing lake levels, future changes in sea levels, and intensity of hurricanes in updating its flood maps. While these provisions respond to our suggestion to Congress, their ultimate effectiveness will depend on their implementation by FEMA. It is too early to evaluate such efforts, but we plan to examine NFIP in the near future.

- *Technical assistance to state and local governments.* The federal government invests billions of dollars annually in infrastructure projects that state and local governments prioritize and supervise. These projects have large up front capital investments and long lead

---

[4]The potential losses generated by NFIP have created substantial financial exposure for the federal government and U.S. taxpayers. While Congress and Federal Emergency Management Agency (FEMA) intended that NFIP be funded with premiums collected from policyholders and not with tax dollars, the program was, by design, not actuarially sound. As of November 2012, FEMA owes the Treasury approximately $20 billion—up from $17.8 billion pre-Sandy—and had not repaid any principal on the loan since 2010.

[5]GAO, *Climate Change: Financial Risks to Federal and Private Insurers in Coming Decades Are Potentially Significant,* GAO-07-285 (Washington, D.C.: Mar. 16, 2007).

[6]GAO, *FEMA: Action Needed to Improve Administration of the National Flood Insurance Program,* GAO-11-297 (Washington, D.C.: June 9, 2011).

times that require decisions about how to address climate change to be made well before its potential effects are discernable. We reported in October 2009 that insufficient site-specific data—such as local temperature and precipitation projections—make it hard for state and local officials to justify the current costs of adaptation efforts for potentially less certain future benefits.[7] We recommended that the appropriate entities within the Executive Office of the President develop a strategic plan for adaptation that, among other things, identifies mechanisms to increase the capacity of federal, state, and local agencies to incorporate information about current and potential climate change impacts into government decision making. USGCRP's 2012-2021 strategic plan for climate change science, released in April 2012, recognizes this need by identifying enhanced information management and sharing as a key objective, and USGCRP is undertaking several actions designed to better coordinate that use and application of federal climate science. We have ongoing work related to these issues. In addition, gaps in satellite coverage, which could occur as soon as 2014, are expected to affect the continuity of climate and space weather measurements important to developing the information needed by state and local officials.[8] According to National Oceanic and Atmospheric Administration program officials, a satellite data gap would result in less accurate and timely weather forecasts and warnings of extreme events—such as hurricanes, storm surges, and floods. We have concluded that the potential gap in weather satellite data is a high-risk area and added it to the High Risk List this year.

- *Disaster aid.* In the event of a major disaster, federal funding for response and recovery comes from the Disaster Relief Fund managed by FEMA and disaster aid programs of other participating federal agencies. The federal government does not budget for these costs and runs the risk of facing a large fiscal exposure at any time. We reported in September 2012 that disaster declarations have increased over recent decades to a record of 98 in fiscal year 2011 compared with 65 in 2004. Over that period, FEMA obligated over $80

---

[7]GAO-10-113.

[8]See, for example, GAO, *Environmental Satellites: Focused Attention Needed to Mitigate Program Risks*, GAO-12-841T (Washington, D.C.: June 27, 2012), and *Environmental Satellites: Strategy Needed to Sustain Critical Climate and Space Weather Measurements*, GAO-10-456 (Washington, D.C.: Apr. 27, 2010).

billion in federal assistance for disasters.[9] We found that FEMA has had difficulty implementing longstanding plans to assess national preparedness capabilities and that FEMA's indicator for determining whether to recommend that a jurisdiction receive disaster assistance does not accurately reflect the ability of state and local governments to respond to disasters.[10] In September 2012, we recommended, among other things, that FEMA develop a methodology to more accurately assess a jurisdiction's capability to respond to and recover from a disaster without federal assistance. FEMA concurred with this recommendation.

The federal government would be better positioned to respond to the risks posed by climate change if federal efforts were more coordinated and directed toward common goals. In 2009, we recommended that the appropriate entities within the Executive Office of the President develop a strategic plan to guide the nation's efforts to adapt to climate change, including the establishment of clear roles, responsibilities, and working relationships among federal, state, and local governments.[11] Some actions have subsequently been taken, including the development of an interagency climate change adaptation task force.[12] However, a 2012 NRC report states that while the task force has convened representatives

---

[9]GAO, *Federal Disaster Assistance: Improved Criteria Needed to Assess a Jurisdiction's Capability to Respond and Recover on Its Own*, GAO-12-838 (Washington, D.C.: Sept. 12, 2012).

[10]GAO, *Managing Preparedness Grants and Assessing National Capabilities*, GAO-12-526T (Washington, D.C.: Mar. 20, 2012). See also GAO, *Disaster Response: Criteria for Developing and Validating Effective Response Plans*, GAO-10-969T (Washington, D.C.: Sept. 22, 2010).

[11]GAO-10-113.

[12]Executive Order 13514 on Federal Leadership in Environmental, Energy, and Economic Performance calls for federal agencies to participate actively in the already existing Interagency Climate Change Adaptation Task Force. The task force, which began meeting in Spring 2009, is co-chaired by the Council on Environmental Quality, the National Oceanic and Atmospheric Administration, and the Office of Science and Technology Policy, and includes representatives from more than 20 federal agencies and executive branch offices. The task force was formed to assess key steps needed to help the federal government understand and adapt to climate change.

of relevant agencies and programs, it has no mechanisms for making or enforcing important decisions and priorities.[13]

In May 2011, we found no coherent strategic government-wide approach to climate change funding and that federal officials do not have a shared understanding of strategic government-wide priorities.[14] At that time, we recommended that the appropriate entities within the Executive Office of the President clearly establish federal strategic climate change priorities, including the roles and responsibilities of the key federal entities, taking into consideration the full range of climate-related activities within the federal government. The relevant federal entities have not directly addressed this recommendation.

Federal agencies have made some progress toward better organizing across agencies, within agencies, and among different levels of government; however, the increasing fiscal exposure for the federal government calls for more comprehensive and systematic strategic planning including, but not limited to, the following:

- A government-wide strategic approach with strong leadership and the authority to manage climate change risks that encompasses the entire range of related federal activities and addresses all key elements of strategic planning.

- More information to understand and manage federal insurance programs' long-term exposure to climate change and analyze the potential impacts of an increase in the frequency or severity of weather-related events on their operations.

- A government-wide approach for providing (1) the best available climate-related data for making decisions at the state and local level and (2) assistance for translating available climate-related data into information that officials need to make decisions.

---

[13]NRC, Committee on a National Strategy for Advancing Climate Modeling, Board on Atmospheric Studies and Climate, Division on Earth and Life Sciences, *A National Strategy for Advancing Climate Modeling* (Washington, D.C.: 2012).

[14]GAO, *Climate Change: Improvements Needed to Clarify National Priorities and Better Align Them with Federal Funding Decisions*, GAO-11-317 (Washington, D.C.: May 20, 2011).

- Actions to address potential gaps in satellite data.

- Improved criteria for assessing a jurisdiction's capability to respond and recover from a disaster without federal assistance, and to better apply lessons from past experience when developing disaster cost estimates.

Additional information on this area is provided on page 61 of our 2013 high risk update. [15]

Mitigating Gaps in Weather Satellite Data

For 2013, we are designating a new high-risk area—*Mitigating Gaps in Weather Satellite Data*. We and others—including an independent review team reporting to the Department of Commerce and the department's Inspector General—have raised concerns that problems and delays on environmental satellite acquisition programs will result in gaps in the continuity of critical satellite data used in weather forecasts and warnings. The importance of such data was recently highlighted by the advance warnings of the path, timing, and intensity of Superstorm Sandy.

Since the 1960s, the United States has used both polar-orbiting and geostationary satellites to observe the Earth and its land, oceans, atmosphere, and space environments. Polar-orbiting satellites constantly circle the Earth in an almost north-south orbit providing global coverage of environmental conditions that affect the weather and climate. As the Earth rotates beneath it, each polar-orbiting satellite views the entire Earth's surface twice a day. In contrast, geostationary satellites maintain a fixed position relative to the Earth from a high-level orbit of about 22,300 miles in space. Used in combination with ground, sea, and airborne observing systems, both types of satellites have become an indispensable part of monitoring and forecasting weather and climate. For example, polar-orbiting satellites provide the data that go into numerical weather prediction models, which are a primary tool for forecasting weather days in advance, including forecasting the path and intensity of hurricanes and tropical storms. Geostationary satellites provide frequently-updated graphical images that are used to identify current weather patterns and provide short-term warnings.

---

[15]GAO-13-283.

Polar-orbiting Satellites

For more than 40 years, the United States has operated two separate operational polar-orbiting meteorological satellites systems: the Polar-orbiting Operational Environmental Satellite series, which is managed by National Oceanic and Atmospheric Administration (NOAA)—a component of the Department of Commerce; and the Defense Meteorological Satellite Program (DMSP), which is managed by the Air Force. The government also relies on data from a European satellite program, called the Meteorological Operational (MetOp) satellite series. These satellites are positioned so that they cross the Equator in the early morning, midmorning, and early afternoon in order to obtain regular updates throughout the day.

With the expectation that combining the two separate U.S. polar satellite programs would result in sizable cost savings, a May 1994 Presidential Decision Directive required NOAA and DOD to converge the two programs into a single new satellite acquisition, which became the National Polar-orbiting Operational Environmental Satellite System (NPOESS). However, in the years that followed, NPOESS encountered significant technical challenges in sensor development and experienced program cost growth and schedule delays, in part due to problems in the program's management structure. After several restructurings and recurring challenges, in February 2010, the Executive Office of the President's Office of Science and Technology Policy announced that NOAA and DOD would no longer jointly procure NPOESS; instead, each agency would plan and acquire its own satellite system. Specifically, NOAA, with support from the National Aeronautics and Space Administration (NASA), would be responsible for the afternoon orbit, and DOD would be responsible for the early morning orbit. The U.S. partnership with the European satellite agency for data from the midmorning orbit would continue as planned.

Subsequently, NOAA initiated its replacement program, the Joint Polar Satellite System (JPSS). JPSS consists of a demonstration satellite—called the Suomi National Polar-orbiting Partnership (NPP)—launched in October 2011; two satellites, with at least five instruments planned for each, to be launched by March 2017 and December 2022, respectively; two stand-alone satellites to accommodate three additional instruments; and ground systems for the entire program. The program is currently estimated to cost $12.9 billion. In June 2012, we reported that NOAA and NASA made progress in establishing the JPSS program and in launching and operating the demonstration satellite, but noted that program officials expect there to be a gap in satellite observations before the first JPSS satellite is launched.

Specifically, NOAA officials anticipate a gap in the afternoon orbit from 18 to 24 months between the time that NPP reaches the end of its lifespan and when the first JPSS satellite is fully ready for operational use. We identified other scenarios where the gap could last from 17 to 53 months. For example, the gap would be 17 months if NPP lasts 5 years until October 2016 and JPSS is launched as planned in March 2017 and undergoes a 12-month on-orbit checkout before it is fully operational. Alternatively, if NPP lasts only 3 years—which NASA engineers consider possible due to poor workmanship in the fabrication of the instruments—and JPSS launches 1 year later than currently planned, the gap in satellite observations could reach 53 months. Figure 1 depicts a potential gap in the afternoon orbit.

Figure 1: A Potential Gap in the Afternoon Orbit

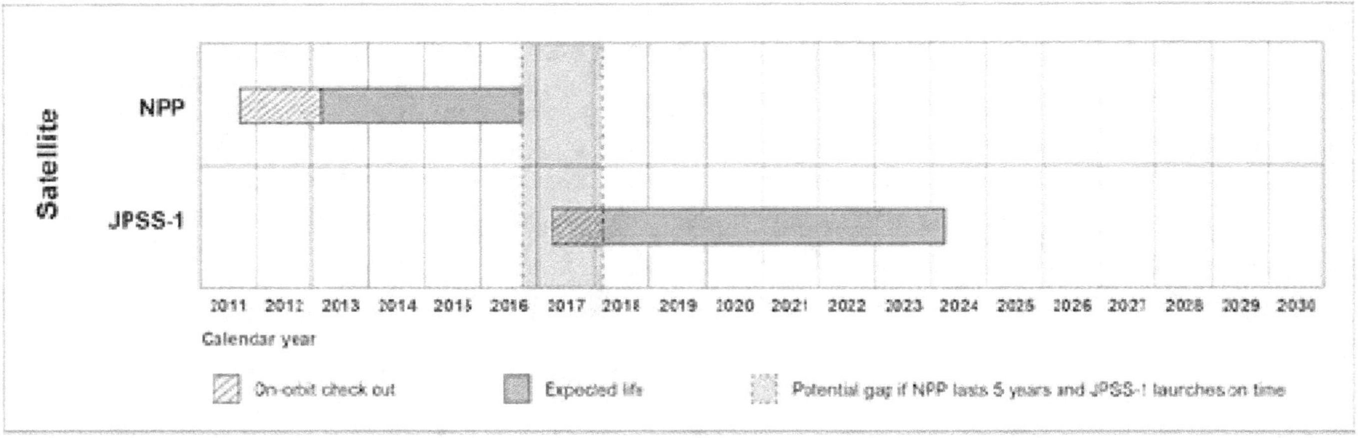

Source: GAO analysis of NOAA data.

After NPOESS was disbanded, DOD also began planning its own follow-on polar satellite program. However, it halted work in early 2012 because it still has two legacy DMSP satellites in storage that will be launched as needed to maintain observations in the early morning orbit. The agency currently plans to launch its two remaining satellites in 2014 and 2020. Moreover, DOD is working to identify alternatives to meet its future environmental satellite requirements. However, in June 2012, we reported that there is a possibility of satellite data gaps in DOD's early morning orbit. The two remaining DMSP satellites may not work as intended because they were built in the late 1990s and will be quite old by the time they are launched. If the satellites do not perform as expected, a data gap in the early morning orbit could occur as early as 2014.

Satellite data gaps in the morning or afternoon polar orbits would lead to less accurate and timely weather forecasting; as a result, advanced warning of extreme events would be affected. Such extreme events could include hurricanes, storm surges, and floods. For example, the National Weather Service performed case studies to demonstrate how its forecasts would have been affected if there were no polar satellite data in the afternoon orbit, and noted that its forecasts for the "Snowmaggedon" winter storm that hit the Mid-Atlantic coast in February 2010 would have predicted a less intense storm further east, with about half of the precipitation at 3, 4, and 5 days before the event. Specifically, the models would have under-forecasted the amount of snow by at least 10 inches. Similarly, a European weather organization[16] recently reported that NOAA's forecasts of Superstorm Sandy's track could have been hundreds of miles off without polar-orbiting satellites—rather than identifying the New Jersey landfall within 30 miles 4 days before landfall, the models would have shown the storm remaining at sea.

In June 2012, we reported that while NOAA officials communicated publicly and often about the risk of a polar satellite data gap, the agency had not established plans to mitigate the gap. At the time, NOAA officials stated that the agency would continue to use existing satellites as long as they provide data and that there were no viable alternatives to the JPSS program. However, our report noted that a more comprehensive mitigation plan was essential since it is possible that other governmental, commercial, or foreign satellites could supplement the polar satellite data. For example, other nations continue to launch polar-orbiting weather satellites to acquire data such as sea surface temperatures, sea surface winds, and water vapor. Also, over the next few years, NASA plans to launch satellites that will collect information on precipitation and soil moisture. Because it could take time to adapt ground systems to receive, process, and disseminate an alternative satellite's data, we noted that any delays in establishing mitigation plans could leave the agency little time to leverage its alternatives. We recommended that NOAA establish mitigation plans for pending satellite gaps in the afternoon orbit as well as potential gaps in the early morning orbit.

---

[16]The European Centre for Medium Range Weather Forecasts is an independent, intergovernmental organization supported by 34 European nations, providing global medium-to-extended range forecasts.

In September 2012, the Under Secretary of Commerce for Oceans and Atmosphere (who is also the NOAA Administrator) reported that NOAA had several actions under way to address polar satellite data gaps, including (1) an investigation on how to maximize the life of the demonstration satellite, (2) an investigation on how to accelerate the development of the second JPSS satellite, and (3) the development of a mitigation plan to address potential data gaps until the first JPSS satellite becomes operational. The Under Secretary also directed NOAA's Assistant Secretary to, by mid-October 2012, establish a contract to conduct an enterprise-wide examination of contingency options and to develop a written, descriptive, end-to-end plan that considers the entire flow of data from possible alternative sensors through data assimilation and on to forecast model performance. In October 2012, NOAA issued a mitigation plan for a potential 14 to 18 month gap in the afternoon orbit, between the current polar satellite and the first JPSS satellite. The plan identifies and prioritizes options for obtaining critical observations, including alternative satellite data sources and improvements to data assimilation in models. It also lists technical, programmatic, and management steps needed to implement these options.

However, these plans are only the beginning. The agency must make difficult decisions on which steps it will implement to ensure that its mitigation plans are viable when needed. For example, NOAA must make decisions about (1) whether and how to extend support for legacy satellite systems so that their data might be available if needed, (2) how much time and resources to invest in improving satellite models so that they assimilate data from alternative sources, (3) whether to pursue international agreements for access to additional satellite systems and how best to resolve any security issues with the foreign data, (4) when and how to test the value and integration of alternative data sources, and (5) how these preliminary mitigation plans will be integrated with the agency's broader end-to-end plans for sustaining weather forecasting capabilities. NOAA must also identify time frames for when these decisions will be made. We have ongoing work assessing NOAA's efforts to limit and mitigate potential polar satellite data gaps.

Geostationary Satellites

Geostationary environmental satellites transmit frequently updated images of the weather currently affecting the United States to every national weather forecast office in the country. These are the satellite images that the public often sees on television news programs. NOAA plans to have its $10.9 billion Geostationary Operational Environmental Satellite-R (GOES-R) series replace the current fleet of geostationary satellites, which will begin to reach the end of their useful lives in 2015.

The GOES-R program has undergone a series of changes since 2006 and now consists of four geostationary satellites and a ground system. However, problems with instrument and ground system development caused a 19-month delay in completing the program's preliminary design review, which occurred in February 2012. In June 2012, we reported that GOES-R schedules were not fully reliable and that they could contribute to delays in satellite launch dates. Program officials acknowledged that the likelihood of meeting the October 2015 launch date was 48 percent.

While NOAA's policy is to have two operational satellites and one backup satellite in orbit at all times, continued delays in the launch of the first GOES-R satellite could lead to a gap in satellite coverage. This policy proved useful in December 2008 and again in September 2012 when the agency experienced problems with one of its operational satellites, but was able to move its backup satellite into place until the problems were resolved. However, beginning in April 2015, NOAA expects to have only two operational satellites and no backup satellite in orbit until GOES-R is launched and completes an estimated 6-month post-launch test period. As a result, there could be a year or more gap during which time a backup satellite would not be available. If NOAA were to experience a problem with either of its operational satellites before GOES-R is in orbit and operational, it would need to rely on older satellites that are beyond their expected operational lives and may not be fully functional. Any further delays in the launch of the first satellite in the GOES-R program would likely increase the risk of a gap in satellite coverage.

In September 2010, we reported that NOAA had not established adequate continuity plans for its geostationary satellites. Specifically, in the event of a satellite failure, with no backup available, NOAA planned to reduce its operations to a single satellite and if available, rely on a satellite from a foreign nation. However, the agency did not have plans that included processes, procedures, and resources needed to transition to a single or foreign satellite. Without such plans, there would be an increased risk that users would lose access to critical data. We recommended that NOAA develop and document continuity plans for the operation of geostationary satellites that included implementation procedures, resources, staff roles, and timetables needed to transition to a single satellite, foreign satellite, or other solution. In September 2011, NOAA developed an initial continuity plan that generally includes these elements. Specifically, NOAA's plan identified steps it would take in transitioning to a single or foreign satellite; the amount of time this transition would take; roles of product area leads; and resources such as imaging product schedules, disk imagery frequency, and staff to execute the changes. In December 2012, NOAA issued an updated plan that provides additional contingency scenarios.

However, it is not evident that critical steps have been implemented, including simulating continuity situations and working with the user community to account for differences in various continuity scenarios. These steps are critical for NOAA to move forward in documenting the processes it will take to implement its contingency plans. Once these activities are completed, NOAA should update its contingency plan to provide more details on its contingency scenarios, associated time frames, and any preventative actions it is taking to minimize the possibility of a gap. We have ongoing work assessing NOAA's actions to ensure that its plans are viable and that continuity procedures are in place and have been tested.

Additional information on this area is provided on page 155 of our 2013 high risk update.[17]

---

[17]GAO-13-283.

Appendix III: Narrowing High-Risk Areas

Management of Federal Oil and Gas Resources

Progress has been made in one of the three areas we identified in our 2011 High Risk List—the Department of the Interior's (Interior) reorganization of its oversight of offshore oil and gas activities.

- *Reorganization.* In October 2011, following the transfer of the Minerals Management Service's oil and gas revenue collection functions to the newly created Office of Natural Resources Revenue, Interior established two new bureaus to provide oversight of offshore resources and operational compliance with environmental and safety requirements. The new Bureau of Ocean Energy Management (BOEM) is responsible for leasing and approval of offshore development plans while the new Bureau of Safety and Environmental Enforcement (BSEE) is responsible for lease operations, safety, and enforcement. Because the responsibilities of these two bureaus are closely interconnected and depend on effective coordination, Interior developed memoranda and standard operating procedures to define roles and responsibilities and facilitate and formalize coordination. Interior also enacted numerous policy changes intended to improve its oversight of offshore oil and gas activities, such as new requirements and policies designed to mitigate the risk of a subsea well blowout or spill. In July 2012, we concluded that Interior has fundamentally completed its reorganization of its oversight of offshore oil and gas activities.

In ongoing and future reviews, our primary focus will be to assess Interior's remaining challenges to managing oil and gas resources—revenue collection and human capital. In so doing, we will also continue to consider Interior's reorganization and its effect on the agency's ability to oversee federal lands and waters.

- *Revenue collection.* In 2008, we reported that Interior collected lower levels of revenues for oil and gas production than all but 11 of 104 oil and gas resource owners whose revenue collection systems were evaluated in a comprehensive industry study—these resource owners included many other countries as well as some states. We recommended that Interior (1) undertake a comprehensive reassessment of its revenue collection policies and processes and (2) establish a balance between collecting revenues and ensuring that public lands and waters remain an attractive option for oil and gas development. In response to our recommendation, Interior contracted for a study called "Comparative Assessment of the Federal Oil and Gas Fiscal System" with the goal to inform decisions about federal lease terms, such as royalties, by consistently comparing the federal oil and gas fiscal systems with those of other countries and identifying ways to increase revenues and improve diligent development. Interior completed this study in October 2011 but Interior is still in the process of deciding if and how to use the results of the study to alter its lease terms. In addition, Interior continues to work to implement a number of our recommendations directed at improving Interior's ability to conduct oil and gas production verification inspections. Finally, Interior is working to implement our recommendations to correct numerous problems with it's efforts to collect data on oil and gas produced on federal lands, including missing data, errors in company-reported data on oil and gas production, sales data that did not reflect prevailing market prices for oil and gas, and a lack of controls over changes to the data that companies reported. We are currently engaged in a review of Interior's revenue collection practices that will evaluate, among other things, Interior's progress in addressing our recommendations.

- *Human capital.* We have reported that the bureaus responsible for oversight and management of federal oil and gas resources on federal lands and in federal waters—Bureau of Land Management (BLM) and the Minerals Management Service (the predecessor to BOEM and BSEE)—have encountered persistent problems in hiring, training, and retaining staff. For example, in 2010, we found that both BLM and the Minerals Management Service experienced high turnover rates in key oil and gas inspection and engineering positions, potentially affecting their oversight of oil and gas development on federal leases. For fiscal years 2012 and 2013, Congress provided funds to BOEM and BSEE in the Gulf of Mexico to establish higher minimum rates of pay for key positions—chiefly geophysicists, geologists, and petroleum engineers—for up to 25 percent of the usual minimum rate of pay. BOEM and BSEE officials in the Gulf of Mexico told us that the pay increase reduced attrition rates for these positions. However, it is uncertain how Interior will address staffing shortfalls to oversee offshore resources in the long term. In July 2012, we reported that Interior was creating a new training program for its inspection staff (such as BSEE's National Offshore Training Program to train inspectors and engineers), but that it may take up to 2 years before new inspection staff are fully trained. Further, human capital issues also exist at BLM and the management of onshore oil and gas. For example, BLM faces similar challenges in hiring, training, and retaining staff for key positions but Interior has not received congressional approval or funds to establish higher minimum rates of pay for these positions as did BOEM and BSEE. We are currently engaged in a review of Interior's efforts to meet its human capital challenges. As part of this effort, we will focus on the causes of

Interior's human capital challenges, actions taken, and how Interior plans to measure the effectiveness of corrective actions.

Additional information on this area is provided on page 76 of our 2013 high risk update. [1]

DOE's Contract Management for the National Nuclear Security Administration and Office of Environmental Management.

To recognize progress at the Department of Energy (DOE) on the National Nuclear Security Administration's (NNSA) and Office of Environmental Management's (EM) execution of nonmajor projects—projects with values of less than $750 million—we are shifting the focus of its high-risk designation to major contracts and projects executed by NNSA and EM, those contracts and projects with values of $750 million or greater. Two of our reviews completed in 2012 focused on nonmajor projects found that these projects were being completed in large part, although additional and sustained attention by DOE is needed to adequately set and document performance baselines and further demonstrate that these actions result in improved performance. These reports included recommendations to DOE to clearly define, document, and track the scope, cost, and completion date targets for each of its projects, as required by DOE's project management order. DOE agreed with these recommendations and plans to apply lessons learned from successful EM projects to its broader portfolio of projects and activities. With further monitoring of this area to ensure that progress is sustained, coupled with continued efforts and commitment by top leadership to address contract and project management weaknesses, nonmajor project performance issues will have been sufficiently addressed.

DOE continues to demonstrate strong commitment and top leadership support for improving contract and project management in EM and NNSA, building on its corrective action plan developed in 2008. In December 2010, the Deputy Secretary convened a DOE Contract and Project Management Summit to discuss strategies for additional improvement in contract and project management. The participants identified six barriers to improved performance and reported in April 2012 on the status of initiatives to address these barriers. In addition, DOE has continued to release guides for implementing its revised order for Program and Project Management for the Acquisition of Capital Assets (DOE O 413.3B), such as for cost

[1] GAO-13-283.

estimating, using earned value management, and for forming project teams. Further, DOE has taken steps to enhance project management and oversight by requiring peer reviews and independent cost estimates for projects with values over $100 million and by improving the accuracy and consistency of data in DOE's central repository for project data.

Challenges remain for the successful execution of major projects. NNSA and EM are currently managing 10 major projects with combined estimated costs totaling as much as $65.7 billion. We have continued to document significant cost increases and schedule delays as well as technical challenges impacting project design. NNSA is tasked with modernizing the nation's aging nuclear weapons production facilities, a challenging effort that will take years and cost billions of dollars. EM faces ongoing complex and long-term challenges in removing radioactive and hazardous chemical contaminants—left over from decades of weapons production—from soil, groundwater, and facilities. Billions of dollars have already been spent, and will continue to be spent over the coming decades to treat and dispose of this waste. In recognition of the significance of these challenges, particularly in a time of fiscal constraint, in 2012, multiple committees of the Senate and House of Representatives held oversight hearings focused on needed improvements to DOE contract management and project performance. Further, the *National Defense Authorization Act for Fiscal Year 2013* includes provisions significant to considerations about NNSA contract and project management, such as cost containment provisions for two of NNSA's largest construction projects, both of which have experienced cost and schedule delays; a requirement that NNSA submit to Congress reports including expected cost savings associated with the award of contracts to manage and operate NNSA facilities; and creation of an advisory panel to make recommendations on revising the governance of the nuclear security enterprise. Until DOE can consistently demonstrate that recent changes to policies and processes are resulting in improved performance on major projects, NNSA and EM will remain on the High Risk List.

Additional information on this area is provided on page 218 of our 2013 high risk update.[2]

---

[2]GAO-13-283.